Readabout

Fire

Written by Stephanie Connell
and Vivienne Driscoll

Macdonald Educational

Fire is very important in our lives. We would
find it difficult to live without fire.

Fire is used to heat our homes and cook our food.
And it gives us light when it is dark. It has a
very important part to play in the way we live.

There are times when we have to fight fire. But
as well as being of use it can also be our enemy.
When a fire is out of control it can destroy
everything in its path. Every year fires destroy
hundreds of houses and buildings and great areas
of forests and heaths. Fires kill and injure many
people and animals every year.

Long ago people lived without fire. They had not found out how they could make fire. They did not know the uses of fire. They ate their food raw. They were cold at night. If a fire was started by lightning they were frightened. They did not know what had happened.

Perhaps one day somebody managed to take a burning
branch from a tree struck by lightning. He could
use the branch to start his own fire. It would
keep his family warm and they would start to cook
their food on it. The fire also frightened away
wild animals.

Then people learned how to make fire when they needed it. They rubbed two sticks together very fast. The sticks got hotter and hotter and started to glow. As they rubbed the sticks they blew on them and the glowing wood burst into flame.

Later they found another way of making fire. They twisted a stick in the hole of a piece of wood. They twisted the stick with the help of a piece of string. The stick was hollow so they could blow through it at the same time.

6

People tried to find an easier way to make fire.
Rubbing sticks and wood was very hard work. One
way they discovered was to strike a piece of steel
against a flint to make a spark. The spark set
fire to dry cloth or bark which was called tinder.

Today we use matches to make fire. The end of the
match is dipped in chemicals that burst into flame
when struck on the special strip on a matchbox.

Tinder box

Matches

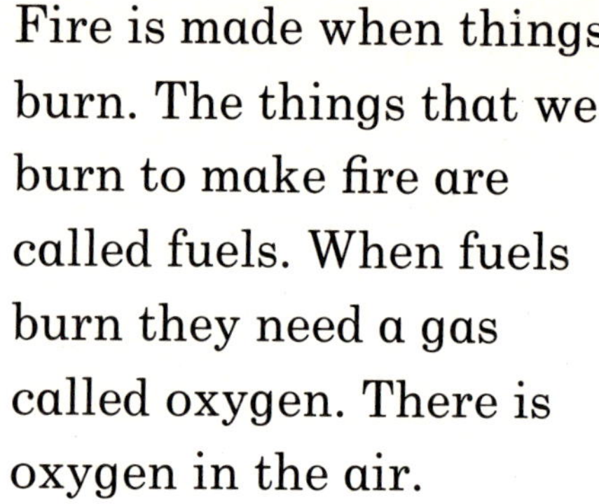

Fire is made when things burn. The things that we burn to make fire are called fuels. When fuels burn they need a gas called oxygen. There is oxygen in the air.

A candle burns using the oxygen that is in the air. If you put a jar over the candle it will soon go out. It uses up all the oxygen that is in the air inside the jar.

When fire burns very quickly there is an explosion.

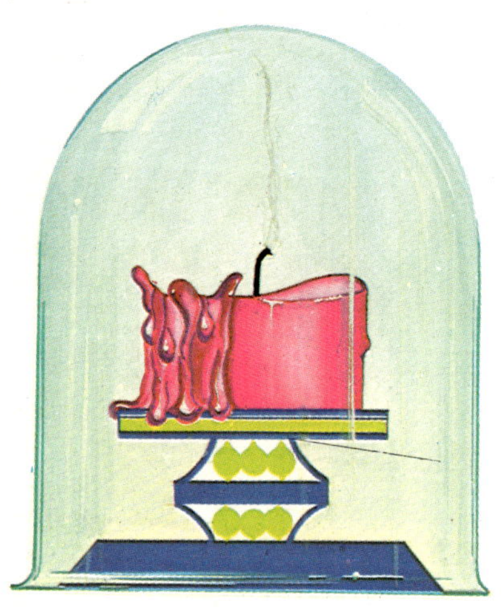

Things that burn so quickly that they make an
explosion are called explosives. When explosions
are controlled by man they can be useful. It is
much easier to blow up a bridge or building that
is no longer needed than to pull it down bit by
bit. The explosives are carefully arranged by
engineers so that they do not damage anything else.
Explosives are often used in mines too.

One of the most important
fuels that we use is coal.
Coal has been forming in
the earth for many millions
of years. Long ago when
the trees died they were
covered by mud and sand.
As the layers built up
the mud and sand pressed
down on the trees and they
were turned into coal.

Coal is found in many places all over the world.
Some coal is near to the top of the ground and is
easy to dig up. But most coal is found deep under
the ground. Miners sink deep shafts to find the
coal seams. Tunnels are dug leading out from the
shaft. The miners cut the coal out as they dig
the tunnels further and further from the shaft.
There are often railways in the tunnels too. They
are used to take the coal back to the shaft. Lifts
are used to carry the coal up to the top.

Another important fuel is oil. Oil is made from the bodies of tiny animals and plants that lived millions of years ago. The oil is found in sand in between layers of rock deep under the ground. To reach the oil men have to drill wells. The oil rises to the surface and it can be collected at the drilling rig.

Oil is used to run many different things. It is used for motor cars, aeroplanes, ships and many other machines.

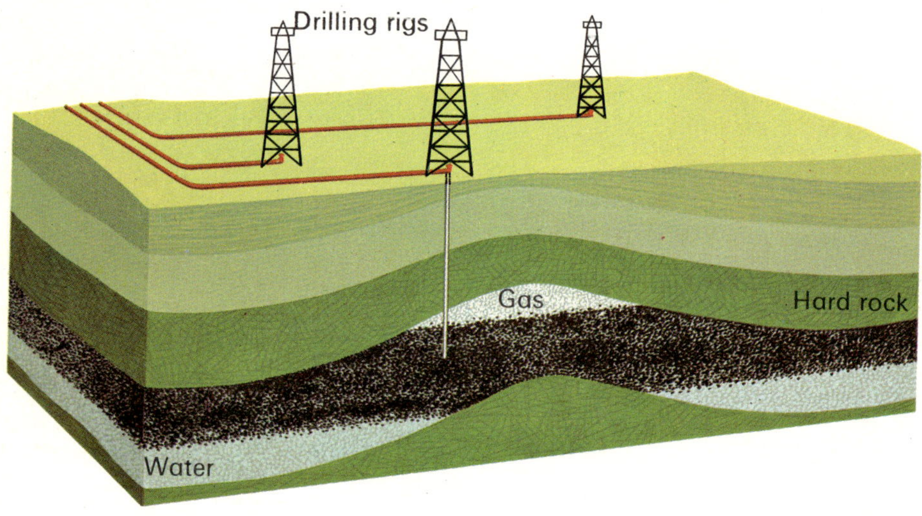

Gas is also an important fuel. Gas is found under
the ground just like oil and coal. Sometimes oil
and gas are found together or very close to each
other. They are sometimes found under the seabed.
Floating drilling rigs are built to get the oil
and gas from under the sea. It is carried to the
land by pipelines. If the rigs are far from land
the oil and gas are loaded onto ships and taken
to a port.

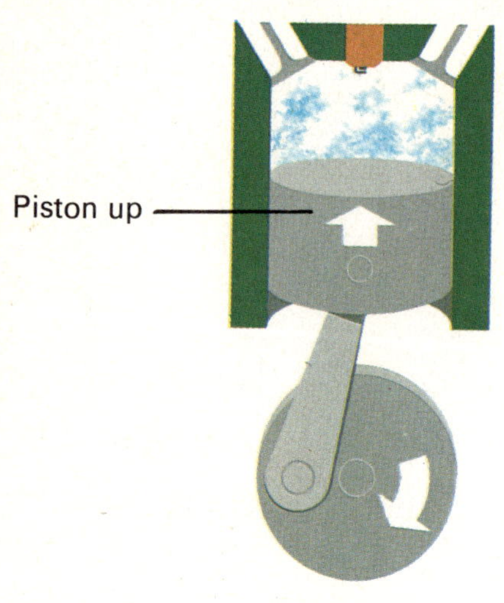

Many engines are run by burning fuel to make power.

In a car engine a mixture of petrol and air is drawn into the cylinders. The pistons travel up the cylinders squeezing the petrol and air mixture to the top. Then the mixture is burned or ignited by a spark from the sparking plugs. The mixture explodes and pushes the piston down. The piston turns a shaft which makes the wheels go round.

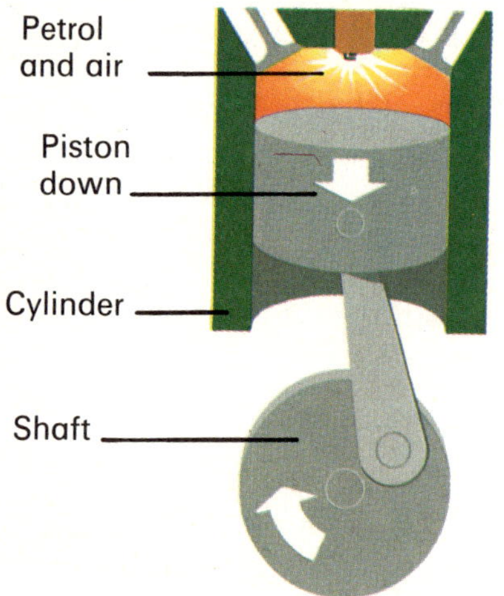

14

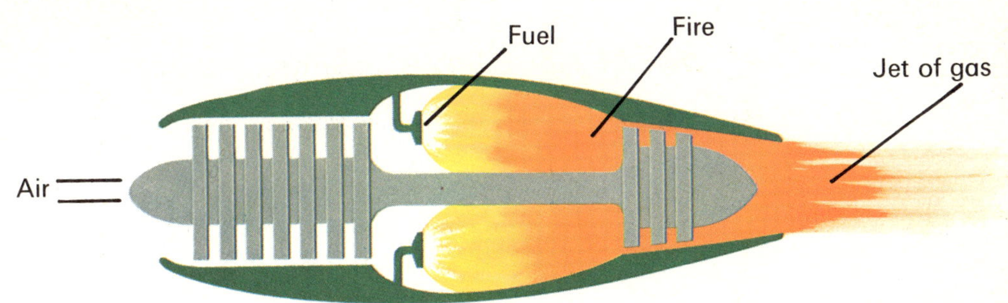

An aircraft jet engine works by burning its fuel in air sucked in from the atmosphere. Hot gases are produced. These shoot backwards from the engine and drive the aircraft forward.
A rocket engine works in much the same way. It produces hot gases which drive the rocket forward. But it carries its own supply of oxygen with it. Rockets fly into space where there is little or no oxygen. If the rocket did not carry its own oxygen the fuel would not burn.

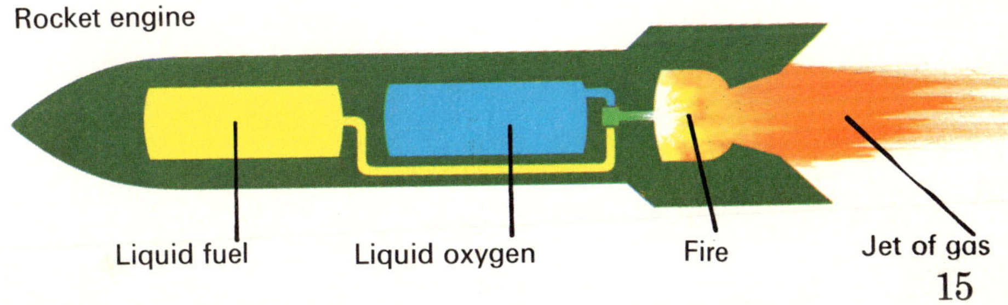

15

Fire is also used to make electricity. The electricity is made at power stations and then is sent by cables to homes and factories.

In a power station fuel is burned in a furnace under a boiler full of water. The heat from the fire boils the water and turns it into steam. The steam is used to drive a turbine, which is like a windmill driven by steam.

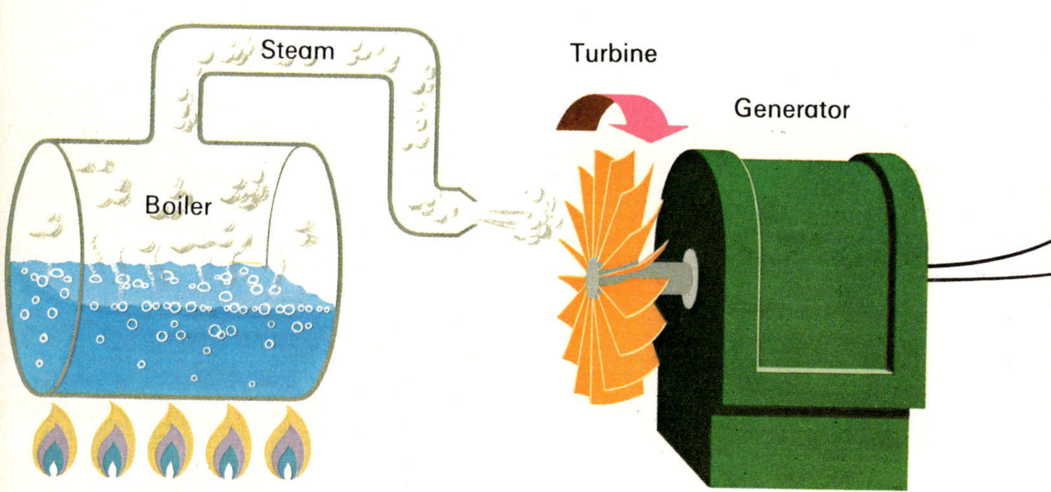

The steam makes the turbine spin round very fast.
Then the turbine drives a machine called a
generator, which makes or generates electricity.
The electricity is carried to our homes along
cables. The cables are carried across the country-
side by pylons. Some electricity cables run along
under the ground. In our homes the electricity is
used for heating and lighting and for running other
electrical machines.

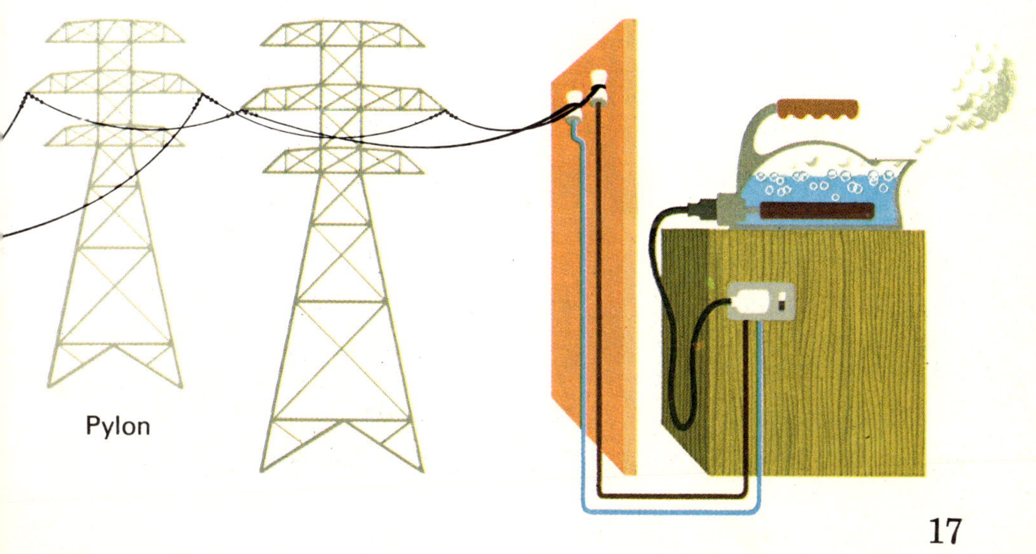

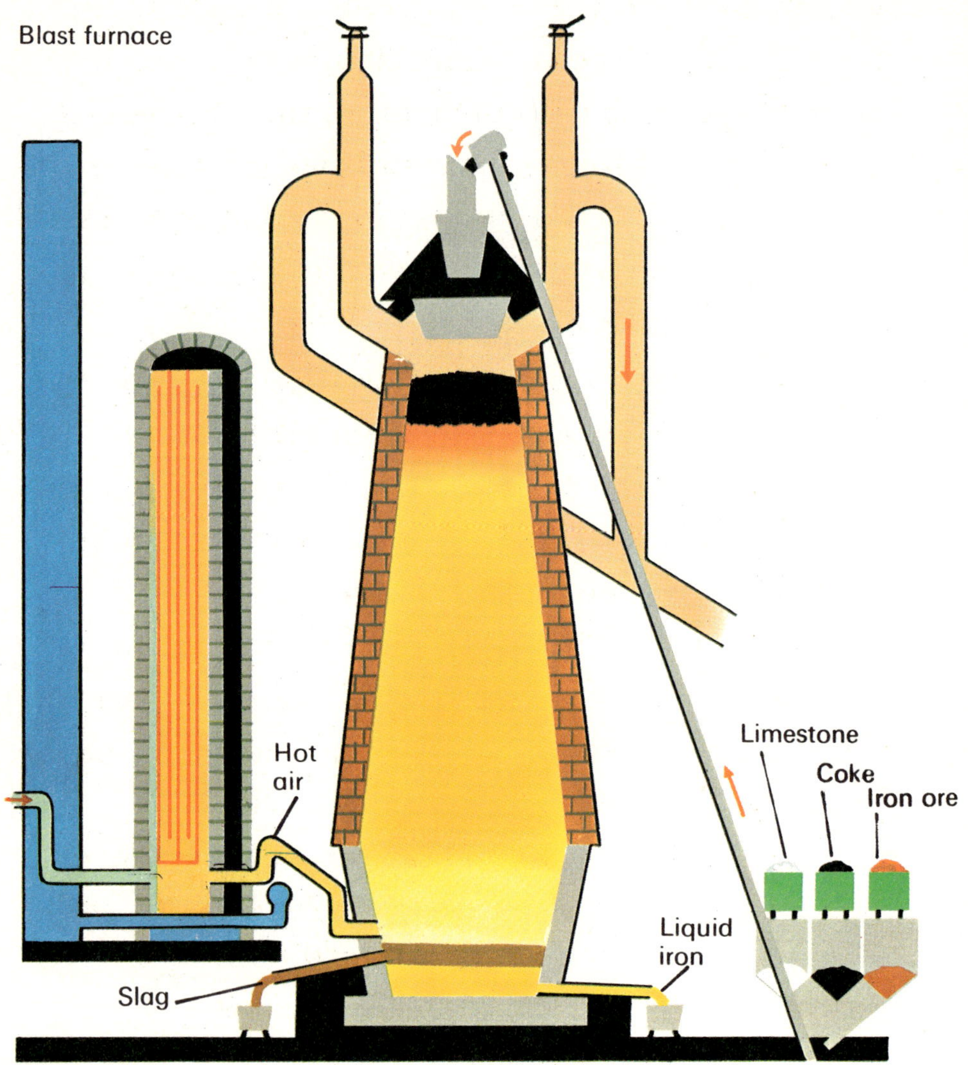

Blast furnace
Hot air
Slag
Limestone
Coke
Iron ore
Liquid iron

When fires reach very high temperatures they can
melt metals and rocks. Many metals are found in
rocks. Rocks with a lot of metal in them are called
ores. If we want to use the metals we must find a
way of getting them from the ores. To do this the
ore is burnt in a furnace at a very high temperature.
This is called smelting.

Iron ore is smelted in a blast furnace. It is
called a blast furnace because hot air is blasted
through it to burn the fuel. Iron ore is poured
into the top of the furnace with a mixture of coke
and limestone. The coke burns at such a high
temperature that the iron ore melts. The liquid
iron sinks to the bottom of the furnace. The rest
of the ore mixes with the lime from the limestone.
This mixture is called slag. The slag floats on
top of the molten iron. The slag and the molten
iron are taken from the bottom of the blast furnace.

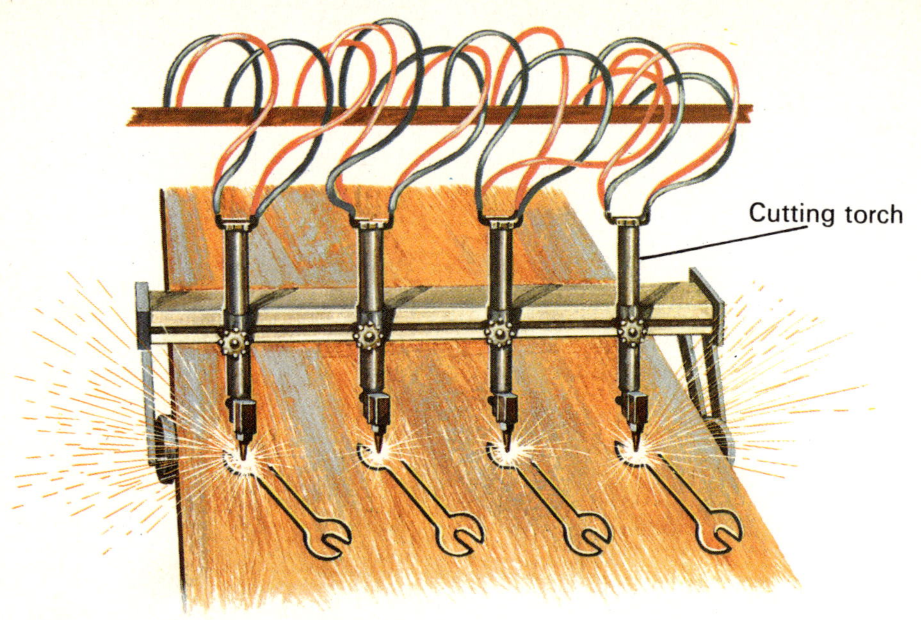

As well as using fire to melt metals we can use it to cut metals. To cut metal we use a cutting torch. In a cutting torch a gas is burned with oxygen to make a very hot flame. The flame is moved over the piece of metal until it is red hot. Then oxygen only is blown on the red hot metal. The metal burns in the oxygen until it is cut. The cutting torch can be held in the hand or fixed to a machine that can cut metals.

20

As well as cutting metal,
gas torches can also be
used to join, or weld,
pieces of metal together.
There is no separate jet
of oxygen in a welding
torch. The gases burn at
a very high temperature.
The ends of the metals
that are to be joined
together are heated until
they melt and mix
together. When the metals
cool again they are joined
together. Welding can also
be done by using an electric
spark, or arc, to melt the
metals.

Welding

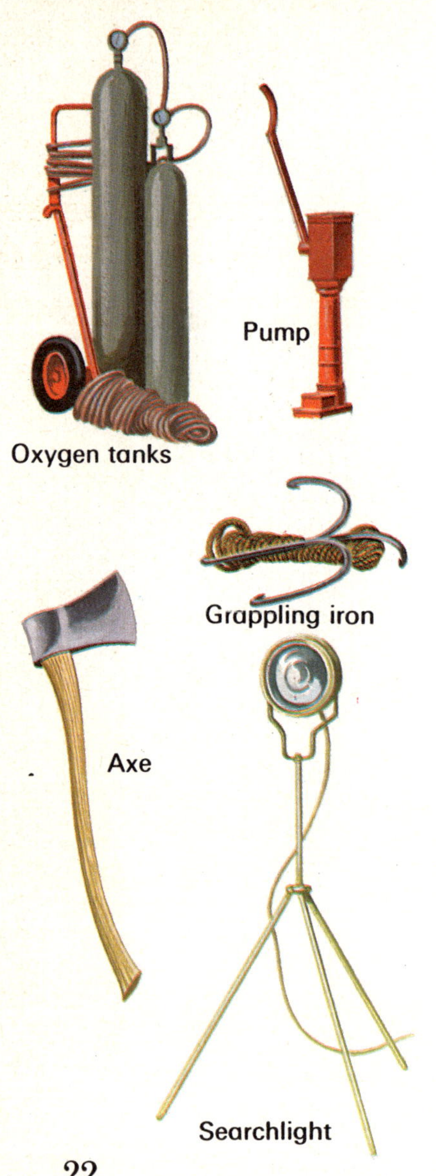

Fires can be very dangerous as well as useful. Fire brigades are called to put out fires that are out of control. When a fire alarm rings at the fire station the firemen drive to the fire as quickly as possible. They ring the sirens on their engines to warn people that they are coming. Firemen wear clothing to protect them when they fight the fire. They wear helmets to protect their heads. Their uniforms are very well made to stand up to the hard work that they do. They carry special equipment to help them.

Firemen fight most fires
with water. In the road
there is a water pipe, or
hydrant. The firemen attach
their hoses to the hydrant.
A pump on the fire engine
pumps the water through the
hoses onto the fire. When
the firemen are fighting
a fire in a tall building
they climb the tall ladders
on their fire engines to
help them reach the flames.

Some fires are so big that they cannot be put out with water. One of the worst fires is a gas fire at an oil well. This kind of fire burns very fiercely.

The flaming gas shoots out of the drill hole. The
only way to put the fire out is to close the drill
hole so that no more gas can escape to feed the
fire. To close the hole explosives are used. The
men wear suits made of asbestos. Asbestos will
not burn in the flames. They carry the explosives
to the drill hole through the flames. Then they
blow the hole up so that it fills in and stops
the gas getting out.

Forest fires are also very difficult to fight.
Men called foresters keep watch for fires. They
must try to stop them spreading if they start.
Often the fires start in the middle of thick
forests where there are no roads and no water.
Aeroplanes are used to spray a mixture of water
and chemicals on the fire. Men called fire-fighters
may be dropped by parachute.

Often the fire-fighters
make a fire-break to stop
the fire from spreading.
They cut down a band of
trees in front of the fire.
The fire will stop at the
fire-break as there is
nothing else to burn.

Fire extinguisher

All big fires start as little fires. If we can put out the little fires quickly we can prevent a lot of damage.

In most large buildings there are things to help us put out the little fires. There may be buckets of sand and water. There may be fire extinguishers. They produce a jet of water, foam or gas that covers anything burning and puts the flames out. Many of the things that we use to fight fire work because they stop the oxygen reaching the flames.

Many factories, offices and large shops have
sprinkler systems to stop fires from spreading.
Every room has a system of water pipes in the
ceiling. In the pipes are special valves that open
when the room gets too hot. When a fire starts,
the heat opens the valves. This lets the water
fall onto the fire and puts it out before it has
spread very far.

There is fire in the sky as well as on the earth.
The sun is like a very hot furnace. The temperatures
are so high that it is difficult for us to imagine
how hot it is. It does not burn in the ordinary way,
with oxygen. It is like a large ball of gases. The
gases are very hot and send out light and heat.
Large flames leap from the sun all the time.

During thunderstorms the sky is often lit by
streaks of lightning. Lightning is an electric
spark which travels from the clouds to the earth,
or between clouds. Sometimes at night you may
see streaks of fire in the sky. They are meteors or
shooting stars. They are pieces of rock which burn
as they travel through the atmosphere.

Index

This is a list of some of the most important words in the book with
page numbers to tell you where to find them. The words which label the
pictures are not in the list.